ABOUT THIS GUIDE

Backyard Birdwatching in Boston is an all-in-one resource for residents of eastern Massachusetts who want to attract and identify common backyard birds. With overviews of birding, gardening, housing, and feeding, this guide is perfect for beginning and experienced birders in the Boston area.

RESOURCES

- Delve into the fascinating lives of birds. Take your knowledge deeper by exploring the Cornell Lab's **All About Birds** website. Visit **AllAboutBirds.org**
- **eBird**'s online species maps are a great way to discover birding hotspots and find out where birds have been seen. Zoom in and start exploring at **eBird.org/explore**
- The **Merlin® Bird ID** app helps you identify your mystery bird. Answer five questions or upload a photo for Merlin to identify. It's free at **Merlin.AllAboutBirds.org**
- Make your garden friendly to birds in every season. How can native plants attract a wider variety of birds? Why are birdbaths important? Answer these questions and explore other helpful topics at **AllAboutBirds.org/gardens**
- **NestWatch** is an international citizen-science project focused on quantifying the breeding success of birds. Learn how to participate at **NestWatch.org**, where you can also find a wide range of online resources for bird enthusiasts interested in learning about birds in the home.
- Join a **citizen-science project**. Scientists need your help to track how birds are faring at locations across the globe. Visit **Birds.Cornell.edu/CitizenScience**

TheCornellLab of Ornithology

WATERFORD PRESS

This guide is based on the All About Birds Pocket Guide Series from the Cornell Lab of Ornithology and Waterford Press. The Cornell Lab is a world leader in the study, appreciation, and conservation of birds. Our hallmarks are scientific excellence and technological innovation to advance the understanding of nature and to engage people of all ages in learning about birds and protecting the planet.

Colors and markings may be duller or absent during different seasons. The measurements denote the length of birds from bill to tail tip. Illustrations are not to scale.

Waterford Press produces reference guides that introduce novices to nature, science, travel and languages. Product information is featured on the website: **www.waterfordpress.com**

Published by Waterford Press.
Text by the Cornell Lab of Ornithology,

© Cornell University 2019.
Bird illustrations © Pedro Fernandes.
Blue Jay cover image © Shutterstock.
Photographs are © as credited; uncredited photos © Shutterstock. All rights reserved.

To order or for information on custom-published products, call 800-434-2555 or email info@waterfordpress.com

Made in the USA

ISBN 978-1-62005-355-3
$9.95 U.S.
50995
9 781620 053553
UPC
8 84682 01338 7
10 9 8 7 6 5 4 3 2 1
807401

TheCornellLab of Ornithology

BACKYARD BIRDWATCHING *in* Boston

AN INTRODUCTION TO BIRDING AND COMMON BACKYARD BIRDS OF EASTERN MASSACHUSETTS

T0123974

BIRDING BASICS

LEARN THE FOUR KEYS TO IDENTIFICATION

In that moment of excitement when you spot a new bird, it's tempting to focus on plumage details called "field marks." However, since plumage varies by the age and gender of the bird, and by the season in which you see it, this is not the most reliable starting point. Start by learning to quickly recognize the group in which your bird belongs. You do this in two ways: by becoming familiar with the general shape, color, and behavior of birds; and by learning what kinds of birds are most likely to be seen in what kinds of habitats and at what times of year. Of course you'll need to look at field marks—a wingbar here, an eyering there—to confirm some IDs. But these four keys will quickly get you to the right group of species, so you'll know exactly which field marks to look for.

1. **SIZE AND SHAPE:** Look at the bird's overall shape and size. Is the bill long or short? How long is the tail? Even subtle differences in head shape, neck length, and body shape can yield useful insights if you study them carefully.

2. **COLOR PATTERN:** Take in the overall pattern of light and dark and note the main colors as well. Some birds have very fine differences that take practice even to see at all. But don't start looking for those details until you've used overall patterns to guide your identification.

3. **BEHAVIOR:** Notice how your bird is sitting, feeding, or moving, whether it's in a flock, and if it has any nervous habits such as flicking its wings or bobbing its tail. When you learn these habits, you can recognize many birds the same way you notice a friend walking in a crowd.

4. **HABITAT:** Habitat is both the first and last question to ask yourself when identifying a bird. You can fine-tune your expectations by taking geographic range and time of year into consideration. You can explore online species maps and seasonal ranges at **eBird.org/explore**

TOOLS FOR BIRD WATCHING

Bird watching is an affordable hobby that you can enjoy virtually anywhere. Beginners really only need an ID guide, quality binoculars, a notepad, and some patience to learn about the birds around them.

Here are the basics to starting your birding hobby:

1. Select the best binoculars that you can afford, taking into account magnification (8X offers good magnification and a wide view), close-focus distance, and weight.

2. Choose a good visual reference guide. It is best to have a portable guide to the birds of a given area to carry in the field. The images in the guide are important, and the descriptive text will help you learn distinguishing features. Download the **Merlin® Bird ID** app to help with identification.

3. Discover other resources that will help you learn more about birds. Join local birding groups and citizen-science projects, such as **eBird**, to help contribute to our understanding of the importance of birds and their role in our ecosystem.

BIRD-FRIENDLY GARDENING

The first step in designing a bird-friendly yard or garden is to evaluate your yard from a bird's perspective. Does it provide the basic necessities—food, water, shelter—that birds need to survive? Putting forth a little extra effort to incorporate the right types of trees, plants, and shrubs will create a more natural environment that is both aesthetically pleasing and highly functional as a habitat for birds and other wildlife. Learn more at **allaboutbirds.org/gardens**

FOOD

Although some bird species will eat from feeders, landscaping your yard to nurture bird-friendly plants creates a more diverse and sustainable environment that will help both migratory and year-round residents survive and reproduce.

WATER

A good source of clean water will draw birds like a magnet. Even a common birdbath purchased at a garden supply shop will do.

SHELTER

Whether it's protection from the elements, safe places to hide from predators, or secure locations for nests, providing shelter is one of the best ways to make your property bird friendly. The more types of food and shelter your yard offers, the more species of birds you will attract.

CREATE A VISUALLY PLEASING BIRDSCAPE

- **Select plants native to your region.** Online tools offer information on size and growth expectations, which influence placement and spacing.
- **Mix woody and non-woody plants.** Woody plants bring interest and structure as the seasons change and herbaceous plants grow and die around the woody ones.
- **Space plants wisely.** Don't overcrowd or leave unexpected gaps.
- **Massing and drifting.** Planting larger clumps of single varieties will attract birds and pollinators because of the efficient foraging they offer, making them smart for wildlife, too.
- **Include wildlife-friendly elements.** Feeders, nest boxes, and bee houses are visual indicators about the intentions of your landscape.
- **Think high & low.** Pay attention to nesting patterns of the species you want to attract when spacing your plants.
- **Containers, structures, and other objects.** Non-plant materials can go a long way toward defining spaces in your yard.
- **Mow edges or create mowed paths.** Mowing a thin strip along paths, like streets and sidewalks, can transform untidy into elegant.

ENCOURAGING NESTING

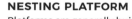

At least 57 species of North American birds nest in boxes or other structures—either purchased or homemade—that meet each species' requirements for a safe place to construct a nest and nurture eggs and nestlings. Here are six ways to add nesting structures to your property:

NEST BOXES

A traditional nest box is intended for cavity-nesting birds and is generally enclosed with four walls, a roof, and a floor. This mimics a hole in a dead tree, which is the natural nest box. Boxes should be the right size for target species. Typical species that use nest boxes include bluebirds, swallows, wrens, chickadees, nuthatches, titmice, and certain ducks and owls.

NEST SHELF

Frank Colver

The nest shelf is designed for species that prefer support from below as well as overhead cover. You might find such species commonly nesting on built structures, and the nest shelf can help direct the nesting effort toward a more convenient location. Typical species that use nest shelves include Eastern Phoebe, American Robin, and Barn Swallow.

PSEUDOCAVITY (OPEN CAVITY)

Dick Tuttle

A pseudocavity combines the seclusion of a nest box and the ease of access of a nest shelf. It is preferred by species such as Carolina Wrens and House Finches, and is meant to be installed on a building.

NESTING PLATFORM

Mara Hopps

Platforms are generally built to attract larger species, some of which would typically nest in big dead trees. They can be more stable in severe weather than a large dead tree. They attract species such as Osprey or Great Blue Heron that typically use sticks and twigs to build nests high in open treetops or on human-built utility poles. Placed in water, they can also attract Canada Geese and Mallards.

NEST BASKET

Les Wolf

Mourning Doves make a flimsy nest and can benefit from a supportive structure such as a nest basket. The basket reinforces the nest bottom and will encourage them to nest in more convenient locations (e.g., away from one's potted plants). Place the nest basket in a shady area, securing it with wire to keep it in place.

NESTING CONE

The Great Horned Owl will make its home in a nesting cone, which should be placed at least 15 to 20 feet high in a live deciduous (not pine) tree in a wooded area. The cones can be constructed of chicken wire and tarpaper, and should be placed outdoors in the fall. Owls will locate the nests for use in January.

FEEDERS & FOOD

You can watch birds anywhere, but the easiest place to start is your own backyard.

The national pastime of feeding birds does more than bring wildlife to your window: it offers you the chance to connect with nature and observe the natural world while contributing to bird health and survival.

Offering the right foods and feeders will help you attract diverse species. By providing a safe space for birds in your backyard, you can create habitat to help your favorite feeder visitors.

FEEDER PLACEMENT

Place feeders in a quiet area where they are easy to see, convenient to refill, and close to natural cover, such as trees or shrubs. Evergreens are ideal because they provide thick foliage where birds can take shelter from predators and winter winds.

Be careful not to place feeders too close to cover or jumping-off points for squirrels and cats. A distance of about ten feet is a good compromise.

Place hummingbird feeders in the shade, because sugar solution spoils quickly in the sun. Don't use honey, artificial sweeteners, or food coloring. If bees or wasps become a problem, try moving the feeder.

Orinithologists estimate that some 600 million birds are killed by hitting windows in the United States and Canada each year. Placing feeders close to your windows can help reduce this problem; within three feet is very safe. When feeders are close, a bird leaving the feeder cannot gain enough momentum to do harm if it strikes the window.

FEEDER CARE

Birds can become ill from leftover bits of seeds and hulls that have become moldy or from droppings that have accumulated on feeder trays. Be sure to clean your seed feeders about once every two weeks, more often during times of heavy use or during warm and damp conditions. Mold can grow inside feeders, so take them apart before cleaning. Use a dishwasher on a hot setting or hand wash with soap and boiling water or with a diluted bleach solution. Or soak feeders for one hour in a weak vinegar solution and scrub with a clean bottle brush. Rinse thoroughly and allow to dry completely before refilling.

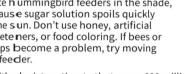

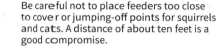

SUNFLOWER SEEDS

Black oil sunflower seeds attract the widest variety of birds and are the mainstay for bird feeders. Other seed varieties will attract different birds to round out your backyard visitors. In general, mixtures of red millet, oats, and other "fillers" are not appealing to most birds and can lead to waste as birds sort through the mix.

DOVES

MOURNING DOVE
Zenaida macroura
To 13.4 in (34 cm)

A plump dove with a long, pointy tail bordered in white. Tan overall with black spots on the wing and peach-colored below. Note thin black bill and pink legs.

ROCK PIGEON
Columba livia
To 14.2 in (36 cm)

Variable in color, most birds are bluish gray with iridescent green-purple neck feathers and two black bands on each wing. The tail is usually dark tipped. Larger and plumper than a Mourning Dove.

WOODPECKERS

DOWNY WOODPECKER ♂
Dryobates pubescens
To 6.7 in (17 cm)

Smaller and with a shorter bill than the Hairy Woodpecker. Note black barring or spots on outer tail feathers. Only the male has a red patch on the head.

RED-BELLIED WOODPECKER ♂
Melanerpes carolinus
To 9.4 in (24 cm)

A medium-sized black-and-white barred woodpecker with a pale belly. Male has a bright red crown and nape, female has only a red nape.

FLYCATCHERS

Yellow-shafted form

NORTHERN FLICKER ♂
Colaptes auratus
To 12.2 in (31 cm)

A large brownish woodpecker with a gray head and white rump patch visible in flight. The undersides of the wing and tail are yellow in the East and red in the West.

EASTERN PHOEBE
Sayornis phoebe
To 6.7 in (17 cm)

A plump songbird that is brownish-gray above and a rich brown head. Female is plain grayish-brown with fine streaking on the belly. Note darker head that is slightly peaked at the rear of the crown.

CROWS & JAYS

AMERICAN CROW
Corvus brachyrhynchos
To 20.9 in (53 cm)

A large, long-legged, thick-necked black bird with a heavy, straight black bill. The short tail is rounded or squared off at the end.

BLUE JAY
Cyanocitta cristata
To 11.8 in (30 cm)

Blue, black, and white overall with a blue crest which they raise when calling. Note white face and throat bordered in black.

BLACKBIRDS & ALLIES

BALTIMORE ORIOLE ♂
Icterus galbula
To 7.5 in (19 cm)

Adult male is flame-orange and black, with a solid-black head and one white bar on black wings. Female and young are yellow-orange on the breast, grayish on the head and back, with two white wingbars.

RED-WINGED BLACKBIRD ♂
Agelaius phoeniceus
To 9.1 in (23 cm)

A stocky blackbird with a conical bill and humpbacked silhouette. Male is black with red-and-yellow shoulder badges. Female is streaked brown with a whitish eyebrow.

BROWN-HEADED COWBIRD ♂
Molothrus ater
To 8.7 in (22 cm)

Male has glossy black plumage and a rich brown head. Female is plain grayish-brown with fine streaking on the belly. Note thick pointed bill.

COMMON GRACKLE ♂
Quiscalus quiscula
To 13.4 in (34 cm)

Male has glossy purple head, bronzy-iridescent body, and yellow eyes. Female is slightly less glossy than male and young birds are dark with dark eyes.

SWALLOWS & SWIFTS

BARN SWALLOW ♂
Hirundo rustica
To 7.5 in (19 cm)

An aerial acrobat that is dark blue above with rufous to tawny underparts and a cinnamon forehead and throat. Note long forked tail on adults in flight.

TREE SWALLOW ♂
Tachycineta bicolor
To 5.9 in (15 cm)

A streamlined swallow with pointed wings and a short, slightly notched tail. Male is blue-green above and white below. Female is brownish above and white below.

CHIMNEY SWIFT
Chaetura pelagica
To 5.9 in (15 cm)

A small, dark gray-brown bird best recognized by its "flying cigar" silhouette. It has a short neck, pale throat, and narrow, curved wings.

CHICKADEES & TITMICE

BLACK-CAPPED CHICKADEE
Poecile atricapillus
To 5.9 in (15 cm)

A tiny, roundish songbird with a black cap and bib separated by stark white cheeks, gray back and wings, and buffy sides and underparts.

TUFTED TITMOUSE
Baeolophus bicolor
To 6.3 in (16 cm)

Steel gray above and white below, with a rusty or peach-colored wash on flanks. Note short bill, large dark eye, and pointed crest.

NUTHATCHES

WHITE-BREASTED NUTHATCH
Sitta carolinensis
To 5.5 in (14 cm)

Compact, short-tailed bird that creeps up and down trees. Gray-blue above and white below with a black cap and a white face. Note chestnut color under the tail.

FINCHES

Breeding ♂   Nonbreeding

AMERICAN GOLDFINCH
Spinus tristis
To 5.1 in (13 cm)

Breeding male is bright yellow with a black forehead and black wings with white markings. Breeding female is dull yellow beneath and olive above. Winter birds are unstreaked and brownish with dark wings and pale wingbars.

HOUSE FINCH
Haemorhous mexicanus
To 5.5 in (14 cm)

Adult male is rosy red around the face and breast, with a streaky brown back, belly, and tail. Note red rump on male in flight. Adult female is plain grayish brown with thick, blurry streaks.

WARBLERS & WRENS

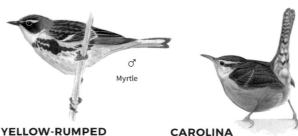

Myrtle

YELLOW-RUMPED WARBLER ♂
Setophaga coronata
To 5.5 in (14 cm)

In summer, male is gray, black, and white with a bright yellow crown, sides, and rump. Female is brownish and less flashy. In winter, birds are pale brown with a yellow rump and pale yellow sides.

CAROLINA WREN
Thryothorus ludovicianus
To 5.5 in (14 cm)

An inquisitive wren, reddish-brown above and warm buffy-orange below, with a long white eyebrow stripe, and white chin and throat. Often holds tail up.

STARLINGS

YELLOW WARBLER ♂
Setophaga petechia
To 5.1 in (13 cm)

Small yellow songbird with a thin, straight bill and a beady black eye. Male is bright yellow overall with reddish streaks down its sides. Female lacks the streaked chest.

EUROPEAN STARLING
Sturnus vulgaris
To 9.1 in (23 cm)

A chunky, blackbird-sized bird with a short tail, iridescent purplish-green plumage, and yellow bill. Introduced to North America from Europe.

THRUSHES & ALLIES

NORTHERN MOCKINGBIRD
Mimus polyglottos
To 10.2 in (26 cm)

Overall gray-brown, paler on the breast and belly, with two white wingbars. Note white patch in the wings in flight. Conspicuous and vocal, mimics other songbirds.

AMERICAN ROBIN
Turdus migratorius
To 11 in (28 cm)

Gray-brown above with a warm orange belly and breast. Note yellow bill, faint streaking on throat, and white eye crescents. Female is similar but paler.

EASTERN BLUEBIRD ♂
Sialia sialis
To 8.3 in (21 cm)

Male is vivid deep blue above with a rusty or brick-red throat and breast and a white belly. Female is grayish above with an orange-brown breast and blue tinges to the wings and tail.

GRAY CATBIRD
Dumetella carolinensis
To 9.4 in (24 cm)

Entirely slaty gray with a darker cap and tail and a rufous-brown patch under the tail. Often hunches its back with its tail tucked downward.

CARDINALS & WAXWINGS

NORTHERN CARDINAL ♂ ♀
Cardinalis cardinalis
To 9.1 in (23 cm)

Male is brilliant red overall, with a thick reddish bill surrounded by black and a red crest. Female is pale brown with warm reddish tinges in the wings, tail, and crest.

CEDAR WAXWING
Bombycilla cedrorum
To 6.7 in (17 cm)

A sleek, pale brown bird with a crest, a black mask, and an affinity for berries. Note yellow-tipped tail.

NEW WORLD SPARROWS

Breeding   Nonbreeding

CHIPPING SPARROW
Spizella passerina
To 5.9 in (15 cm)

In summer, markings are clean and crisp with frosty grayish-white underparts, pale face, and black line through the eye topped off with a rusty crown. In winter, subdued buff brown with a pinkish bill.

AMERICAN TREE SPARROW
Spizelloides arborea
To 5.5 in (14 cm)

Gray head and nape with rusty cap, eyeline, and unstreaked breast with a central dark spot help separate this winter sparrow from others. Note bicolored bill, black above, yellow below.

WHITE-THROATED SPARROW
Zonotrichia albicollis
To 7.1 in (18 cm)

Large, plump sparrow with a bright white throat and yellow spots between eye and bill. Two forms are common: one with black-and-white-striped crown; the other with buff-on-brown-striped crown.

EASTERN TOWHEE ♂
Pipilo erythrophthalmus
To 8.2 in (20.8 cm)

A striking, oversized sparrow with a thick bill and long tail. Male is black above with a black breast, warm rufous sides, and a white belly. Female is similar, but is brown instead of black.

OLD WORLD SPARROWS

Slate-colored form

HOUSE SPARROW ♂
Passer domesticus
To 6.7 in (17 cm)

Male has a gray head, whitish cheeks, black bib, and rufous neck. Female is buffy brown with dingy underparts. Introduced from Europe and not related to other sparrows.

DARK-EYED JUNCO ♂
Junco hyemalis
To 6.3 in (16 cm)

"Slate-colored" form is neat gray on the back, head, and throat with a white belly, pink bill, and white outer tail feathers that flash in flight.